LOFOTEN –

LEIF RYVARDEN

VESTERÅLEN

*Mountain Kingdom
in the Sea*

Photographs by
Jørn Bøhmer Olsen and Rolf Sørensen

Translated by Inger Fluge Mæland

BOKSENTERET

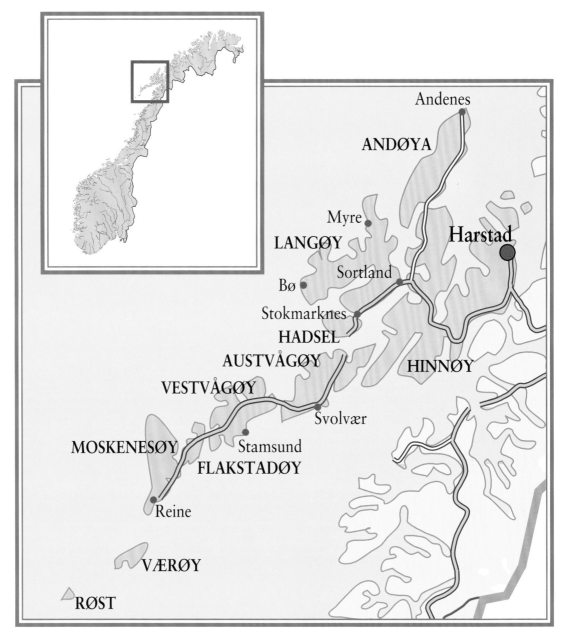

© Copyright: Boksenteret A/S, 1996
Designer: Øyvind Skagmo, Boksenteret A/S
Production: Tangen Grafiske Senter AS, Drammen 1996

ISBN 82-7683-108-7

Published in cooperation with Nortrabooks

Photographs by Jørn Bøhmer Olsen and Rolf Sørensen,
with the exception of the following: Steinar
Haugberg/Samfoto, page 21, Trym Ivar Bergsmo/Samfoto,
page 26, Leif Ryvarden, page 48/49 (bottom), 79 (right),
80, 81 (left), Jogeir Stokland, page 88, 89.

For information, please contact the publisher:

Boksenteret A/S
Postboks 3125 Elisenberg
0207 Oslo
NORWAY
Telephone number: 47 22 54 07 00

*Half-title: Northern lights and stars above Himmeltindan,
Vestvågøy, one of the stateliest and most striking mountains in
Lofoten.*
Title page: Panoramic view of Reine.

CONTENTS

MOUNTAIN KINGDOM IN THE SEA

The Lofoten-Vesterålen archipelago represents some of the most distinctive scenery in all of Norway. Due to its obvious departure from the curved back of the Norwegian coastline, the area is included on even the sketchiest map of Europe. This is indeed the clue to the area's uniqueness – its location far north and out in the ocean.

This is a land of contrasts; whether you approach it from the sea, that immense ocean to the west, or by traveling north along the jagged Norwegian coastline, the impression is always the same: a chain of mountains rising out of the wide blue sea, at a distance a seemingly inhospitable place where rock and snow are the most noticeable features. On approach the impression changes: by the foot of the mountains fields and houses lie scattered on a level green belt, while trees and shrubs clamber up the mountainsides.

Out here in the ocean you will find a changing landscape offering great variety: islands, skerries, and reefs – and wide beaches where you can wade barefoot in the finest white sand or skip along on big boulders polished through millennia of rolling waves. Farther inland the mountain peaks stand in rows, separated by extensive woodland and wide-open moors where nothing can be heard save the wind and the birdsong. Should you arrive in summer, the light will fill your mind; these long restless nights, slumbering only in the filtered light of morning. You are in a fairyland in which you can wander in solitude along shores where the voice of the great ocean fills your ears as the white-bannered waves roll ashore. An hour later you can walk across big snowpacks and enjoy the breathtaking view of a mountain kingdom.

If fishing is your pleasure, the ocean is yours; go ahead and help yourself. Nobody demands to see a fishing license or any such formalities. Miles of hiking trails are waiting for you, sporting the well-established red T's of the Norwegian Mountain Touring Association; and there are huts where you can rest your tender feet and tired back when evening comes and the summer light wanes. If you are a bird watcher, you will find yourself in Norwegian bird heaven, where the eagle is a common sight, where gulls roam by the million, and where puffins and guillemots rush in as if snowshowers from the cliffs.

You are free to enjoy fresh air, clean water, and peace at your leisure, sitting by the campfire by the grand sweep of the seashore or in the quiet comfort of the woods. If you prefer a white tablecloth and sparkling wine, the remedy is close at hand. No more than an hour's travel will take you to hotels that can give you what your heart and tastebuds desire. Between these two extremes you have the choice of accommodations ranging from simple campgrounds to

Left: Eggum, Vestvågøy - a typical Lofoten view. Through millions of years the sea has carved a level shore from the steep mountains. In sheltered areas large sandy beaches formed, but in places facing the ocean all sand and silt have been washed off into deep water, leaving only the boulders behind.

Tourists are not the only residents of fishermen's shanties. Space permitting, the friendly kittiwake often stays at local "cliffs." As you can see, even kittiwakes have to book early in the busy season.

fishermen's shanties where you do your own housekeeping.

The people living here reflect the variety and the contrasts in the landscape, and their generosity matches that of the sea itself. Opinions and attitudes have been shaped through generations of struggle to make a living in this land that not only gives but also takes. The fair and gentle days of summer yield to a dark winter of cold winds and snow, often accompanied by a seething ocean topped by furious waves. Modern weather forecasting and technology have made the ocean a safer, but still a demanding workplace, and fishing remains the mainstay of Lofoten and Vesterålen's contribution to the Norwegian economy. The evidence is everywhere: drying racks for fish, wharfs, fishing nets hung to dry, and all kinds of boats. The whiff of salt water and dried fish is always in the air.

Today there is an excellent network of roads covering Lofoten and Vesterålen, and many ferries have been re-placed by tunnels and bridges. Therefore it is easy to get around by bike or by car. You are the explorer, and there is a lot waiting to be discovered. Leave busy roads behind, seek out hidden coves and inlets, and you will find gems of Norwegian scenery in a beautiful setting of sea and sky.

Should you want to visit a different country, a harsher land, come in winter. The greenish-yellow flickering of the northern lights and the white snow will guide you beneath brilliant starry skies. And if you experience the ocean in the powerful grip of a gale, you will see an incredible display of forces as foamy-white, grayish-green mountains of water are smashed against the land.

Each time of year has its own distinctive features in this mountain kingdom in the sea, so it is up to you to pick those you want to experience. The people and the land are always there to greet you.

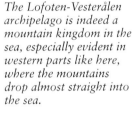

The Lofoten-Vesterålen archipelago is indeed a mountain kingdom in the sea, especially evident in western parts like here, where the mountains drop almost straight into the sea.

ANDØYA

Andøya is one of Norway's most exotic islands, and on your arrival here you will encounter a landscape rarely seen elsewhere in the country. The island is oblong and tapered, with steep mountains at the southern end. To the north it is so low and level that in places the island itself seems to disappear into the ocean. On this elongated pancake are found a number of small, grass-covered peaks, a kind of huge pyramid landscape. The island also has some of Norway's largest bogs, the protected Dverbergmyra being the largest. If you wander through this marshy landscape among cloudberry patches, nodding cotton grass, muddy flats, and winding willow-covered streams, there is only the hum of the breakers in the west to remind you that you are well out in the sea instead of far to the east on the plains of Finnmarksvidda.

The dark green pyramidal mountains welcome hikers and reward them with an unobstructed view, either of the great ocean to the west, or southward towards the summits at Hinnøya. To the north lie Senja and the mountains of Troms with their array of spires and towers.

The large boggy flats are full of birds in the summer, both among the brushwood and on the ponds; and the meadow pipit and the golden plover's melancholy song can be heard wherever you go in this slightly somber landscape. If you can spare only one day here, the best route would be to take the inner road north and the outer one back down. Even in such a short visit you will be able to appreciate the special character of this island.

The Coal Mines at Ramså
The mountains of Norway are very old, but up at Ramså, on the northern part of Andøya, an exception can be found in a formation from the Cretaceous period, "only" 120 million years old. In

The bogs at Dverbergmyra are among the largest in the country. Large areas are nature preserves rich in bird and plant life. With the landowner's permission you can pick cloudberries here in the fall.

The sand at Ramså Fossil Park hides a nice bit of Ice Age history in the form of a buried layer of peat. This was formed once the area dried out as the ice receded. When large quantities of ice thawed, the land was again covered by the sea, and fresh sand was deposited on the old peat layer. In the following millennia the land rose, leaving it all on dry land.

Above right: Peat cutting, very important in earlier times, is now a rather casual pursuit, except at Ramså where a large company produces peat on a commercial basis.

Right: The archipelago has some of the country's largest tidal ranges, and at ebb tide extensive littoral areas are exposed. This is a lugworm's paradise, shown by the many pyramids it makes.

this formation we find the only coal fields in Norway proper and, along with the coal, a number of fine specimens of fossils, such as those of marine reptiles and other animals buried in the plant materials that turned into coal. In the nineteenth century, when authorities learned that the people of Andøya gathered coal along the shores, they started mining on an experimental basis. However, the coal was of poor quality, and the mining operation ended

with the experiment. Today the area has a number of instructional signposts to allow for an interesting self-guided tour, but the mines themselves are for the time being closed to the public.

Near Ramså at Ramsåmyra you will find one of Norway's largest peat-producing operations. The bog used for the purpose looks huge, but it represents a mere five percent of the total marshland

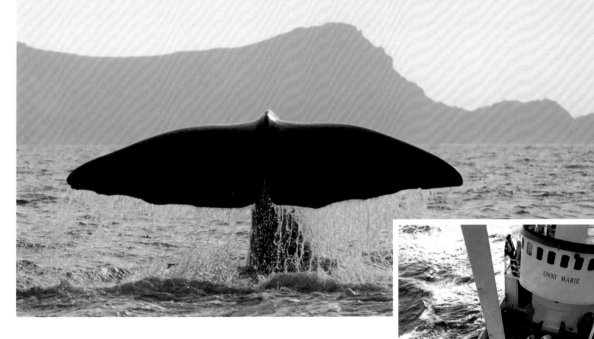

Nowhere else in Europe do you get as close to the whale as off Andøya. The enormous tail of the sperm whale is the last thing you see as the animal starts its deep dive down to three thousand feet, where it finds its favorite food, giant squid. The dive takes less than ten minutes, and it is a physiological feat that remains a mystery.

at Andøya. The peat is primarily used as a growing medium for seedlings, and the plant employs approximately forty full-time workers. This bog alone has enough peat for an estimated thirty years of production.

The Kingdom of the Whale

Nowhere else in Norway is the continental margin, the line between the fishing reefs and the great ocean deep, as close to the coast as at Andenes, and this "edge" is where many species of whales come to feed. In spring a great increase in plankton due to the longer daylight hours brings an abundance of fish, and not only fish, but also a good supply of squid, which is a delicacy to the sperm whale. Just like the migratory birds, the whales travel north every year to gorge themselves on the summer smorgasbord. The rest of the year is spent in subtropical waters, where the young are born. The whales travel in schools, and groups of twenty or thirty are not unusual. As far back as the sixteenth and seventeenth centuries Dutch ships hunted whales in these rich waters, followed by Norwegian ones, a practice that continued until commercial whaling was stopped a few years ago.

It is primarily sperm whales and finbacks that frequent areas near the continental margin, and throughout spring and summer there are excursions out to the "edge" to observe these graceful and impressive animals in their natural element. The Whaling Centre staff are

Whale-watching boats have a proper crow's nest, which nearly always ensures that the crew locate whales. They are so confident of success that if they fail, you get a second trip for free.

Oksebåsen at the nor-
thern tip of Andøya has
our only rocket range.
Here rockets are launched
to study the northern
lights and other atmos-
pheric phenomena.
It was one of these rock-
ets that almost convinced
Russian authorities that
the Third World War had
started.

Next page:

Top: Andenes is the ad-
ministrative hub of And-
øya and has a fine arctic
museum and whale infor-
mation center where
whale-watching excur-
sions start. Fishing and
the military base (back-
ground) provide the main
local sources of income.

Middle: Bleikstranda is
the nation's longest beach
and a good place for soli-
tary walks in wet sand as
you listen to the many
voices of the summer
seas. The strong winds
have carried a lot of sand
up onto the rock wall in
the background, creating
wonderful "hanging"
dunes.

Bottom: Dverberg
Church is an octagonal
wooden structure built in
1843 and nicely situated
by the sea, making it a favorite motif for passing
photographers.

so confident of your seeing whales that
they give you a second excursion for
free if you should miss on the first try.
The excursions are extremely popular,
so during the peak season you are
advised to book ahead.

The Norwegian Rocket Range

Today all technologically advanced
nations have their own rocket range,
and Norway is no exception. Ours is
located in Oksebåsen, a sheltered cove
on the northernmost tip of Andøya.
Here rockets are launched to study
atmospheric phenomena such as the
Northern Lights. With such advanced
technology even peaceful pursuits can
cause potentially serious situations.
This was demonstrated in 1995 in an
incident where miscommunication led
Russian authorities to think that their

radar screens had picked up an enemy
rocket. The alarm went all the way to
President Yeltsin before the misunder-
standing was cleared up and the incident became the object of T-shirt
humor rather than horror.

Norway's Longest Beach

Once you round the northernmost tip
of Andøya, you get to the spectacular
Bleikstranda, almost a mile and a half
long. It has vast areas of shifting dunes
containing an odd mixture of shore and
mountain flora. You may also notice
how flying sand has been blown onto
the steep wall of the mountain beyond,
creating one of the few hanging sand
dunes in Norway. Beyond Bleikstranda
lies the characteristic hood-shaped
Bleiksøya, Andøya's largest bird colony.
From Bleik there are daily boat trips to

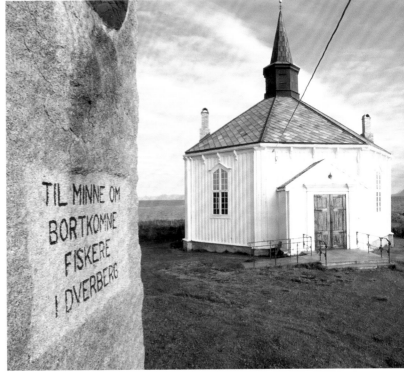

Bleiksøya. During the nesting season you are not allowed to go ashore, but in fact the best view of the colony with all its different species and busy social life can be had onboard the boat. Just like Torghatten at Helgeland, Bleiksøya has a hole running through the island. The fishing hamlet Bleik is also unique in its unusual village-like appearance, with houses built exceptionally close to one another compared to other sparsely populated communities in Norway.

The northern tip of Andøya was probably not covered by the glacier during the last ice age, and in many ways it is a geological treasure trove. Among its treasures is the country's oldest terminal moraine, Hauan, forming a gravel snake that is seventy-five feet high and a mile and a half long. Well-marked trails lead to prominent peaks.

LANGØY

Langøy is difficult to recognize as an island when you arrive here. It is entirely too cut up by narrow fjords and inlets, separated by steep mountains and extensive wetlands, to give an overall impression. Exaggerating just a little, one might say that the island looks like a cloverleaf, divided into three sections, each comprising one municipality, Øksnes to the north, Bø to the west, and Sortland to the east. Good roads make it easy to get around, and bridges connect the island to the neighboring islands of Andøya, Hinnøya, and Hadsel.

Stø

On the northern tip of Langøy lies the fishing hamlet Stø, surrounded by spectacular scenery that keeps the cameras clicking away when the midnight sun bathes land and sea. If you would like a boat trip, in the summer there are daily whale-watching excursions out to the continental margin, where the sperm whales feast at their local larder. These enormous animals make an impressive sight as they move their thirty to seventy tons along the surface of the water, breathing in prep-

Stø at the north end of Langøy is handsomely placed beneath Geitberget. A scenic trail follows the shore towards Nyksund to the west.

aration for their dizzying dives to depths of more than three thousand feet in search of giant squid. They can stay underwater for up to ninety minutes, dropping to the bottom at the rate of more than five hundred feet a minute. It is still a mystery how they manage to find their prey in the total darkness that prevails down there and how they are physically capable of surviving the great changes of pressure in such a short time.

In addition to your trip to see the whales, it is recommended that you follow the marked trail that runs from Stø to the ghostlike abandoned fishing hamlet of Nyksund. The walk offers great scenic experiences, the mountains at your back, all the birds and the ocean's wide arena ahead of you. You can take a break at Skipssanden, a beautiful sandy beach in one of the many coves. There is plenty of driftwood along the shore for making a cup of coffee. If you have the time, you should also treat yourself to a visit to

Anda Lighthouse with its splendid bird cliffs and resident seal population. Should you be in the mood for some deep-sea fishing, it can easily be arranged.

Nyksund – A Shadow of Its Former Self

A bit north of Myre, the administrative center in the municipality of Øksnes, is the turnoff leading to Nyksund. The road alone is a treat, as it winds its way alongside the mountain next to the open sea. Splendid cobble-strewn beaches invite you to stop and explore,

Whale-watching trips are widely available in Vesterålen, thanks to the proximity to the whales' feeding grounds by the continental margin.

Nyksund, once a busy fishing hamlet, is today a decaying ruin - picturesque at times, but not beautiful. There are plans to restore it.

Nykvåg is a tiny fishing hamlet far west in Vesterålen. Nowhere are bird cliffs closer to human habitation.

few weeks on the outskirts of Norway. What makes the local wharfside warehouses special is their two-story structure, designed to cope with the great tidal range. Two levels allowed for more effective loading and unloading. With the changeover to larger fishing boats Nyksund's location on the oceanside of the island became less important, and little by little the entire population of the hamlet moved into Myre. From Myre there are also excursions to neighboring islands. Skogsøya is particularly striking, with its pointed peaks forming a u-shape to shelter a valley that terminates in a fine sandy beach.

Nykvåg – Bird Cliffs Next Door

Traveling from Sortland, or on your trip back from Myre or Stø, at the bottom of Eidsfjorden you will see the summit of Reka to the west. With its razor-sharp, tooth-like shape, it seems to rise in protest against all the other mountains, which have allowed themselves to be worn down by the ravages

and the road ends at Nyksund. Once upon a time this was a busy fishing hamlet, but today the houses are empty and no one lives here any more. The weather has taken its toll on the buildings, but restoration has started, in part with the aid of young people from other European nations who want to spend a

Top, previous page: The shoreline south of Nyksund is a rock collector's eldorado, with plenty to choose from. Inderøya in the background.

Left: The kittiwake is a most trusting gull. It often nests on windowsills or on steep rocks close to buildings.

In the absence of trees the magpie makes do with what is at hand, in this case a telephone line keeps the nest aloft.

Top: Langøy lends support to the idea of a mountain kingdom in the sea. View towards Reka.

Above: South of Nykvåg lie Bufjellet and the peninsula Engenyken, like a hat on the sea.

of time. It takes experience and good climbing gear to make it to the top. Heading west, the road winds between fjord and mountain until you pass through the Ryggesfjell tunnel, the gate to outer Vesterålen and the municipality of Bø.

If you want to see bird cliffs right in the neighborhood without the use of a boat, you turn west towards Nykvåg. Around and almost within this tiny fishing hamlet there are numerous crags and rocks that provide nesting sites for thousands of birds, primarily kittiwakes, which keep you informed of their presence twenty-four hours a day.

Should a gray sea eagle approach the cliffs, the gulls' chorus becomes a cacophony of screeches and screams until the dark shadow disappears once more. Nowhere else in Vesterålen will you see bird cliffs at such close range; you don't need any fancy zoom lenses to take fancy pictures. A short rowing trip out to the island Fuglenyken, about a hundred yards from the hamlet, takes you right up to the grandest bird cliffs in the region, the home of thousands of kittiwakes, guillemots, razorbills, and cormorants, in addition to gulls by the thousand. Following your visit to the bird colonies, head for Hovden along one of the most extensive cobble beaches in Norway. On the beach nature has created a two-mile art gallery consisting of rocks in varying colors and sizes in an endlessly shifting pattern. Not a single stone is identical to another, and words fail to describe the wealth of beauty and perfect form revealed as you wander along, your pockets ever more overloaded with rocks. The wide ocean and the waves' eternal heartbeat against the shore cannot but strengthen the feeling of eternity and of how short our lives really are.

Bird watchers are urged to also make a stop at the wetlands near Straume, known for their rich and varied birdlife, including many waders and ducks.

Føre and Svinøy – the Past Revisited

There have been people in Vesterålen for thousands of years. At Føre, just south of Straume, we find a remarkable burial site that sheds light on earlier inhabitants of the islands. In a small sandy area there are twelve carefully constructed graves from around A.D. 300-400. This is the early part of the

Iron Age, and the various persons have been buried with objects that tell us a lot about their lives and living conditions. The dead were buried in tight stone coffins, and the dry sand has preserved many of their skeletal remains until today. One of the finest examples is the grave of a woman who, among other things, brought along to the afterlife a fine glass beaker that originated in the Cologne area of Germany. It indicates that there was already at that time trading all along the Norwegian coast. The woman was buried wrapped in a bearskin, also a reminder of a bygone era when the Lofoten and Vesterålen archipelago was covered by great forests where bears and wolves

A mild climate and an even rate of precipitation provide fertile farmland wherever the soil is deep enough.

Even to the far west in Vesterålen, where the ocean has a free path, many beautiful beaches can still be found in sheltered bays, as here at Hovden.

roamed. Spend an hour at Føre; visiting this place makes us reflect on times when life was harder and more down to earth than in our technological age.

If you have the time, Svinøy is also worth a visit. It has more than two hundred graves from the later Iron Age, and a historical marker gives you information about the objects found here. Your visit can be combined with a swim at Svinøyvalen, a sandy beach more than a mile long on the leeward side of the island. At low tide you can, in fact, walk across to Svinøy; the inlet between the island and the beach is so shallow.

Hamsun Country

A visit to Bø is a must for anyone interested in the work of the Norwegian author Knut Hamsun. This is where he came at the age of seventeen and got a job, first as a clerical assistant to the local judicial and administrative officer, later as a temporary teacher. Hamsun's inadequate training for either job must have been compensated for by his integrity and imposing figure; and there was nothing wrong with his competence as a storyteller. He lived here for two years, and in his spare time he took his first steps towards becoming a writer, in the books *The Enigmatic One* and *Bjørger*.

The sheriff's residence at Vinje has been restored as a museum and gives you a good idea of what homes looked like at the time when the author wandered through "the never-ending day of a Nordland summer."

Apropos wandering, the Vesterålen Hiking Club has made a very nice network of hiking trails throughout the

Near Malnes in Bø, the westernmost part of Langøy.

area, and the summits are never far off, offering spectacular panoramic views of this extensive archipelago. All through the summer season the hiking club organizes hikes, both straight-forward walks and also topical excursions featuring such subjects as local history or nature. At the tourist information office you can get a program and a map, as well as information on different trips.

Jennestad Country Store

A bit north of the town of Sortland lies the Jennestad Country Store, a reminder of a past when going to the store meant more than a quick run to a self-service supermarket. Jennestad for a long time served as an important crossroads in Vesterålen, but a ferry landing and an improved harbor at Sortland meant that Jennestad gradually lost its importance. It was not just a place of business; it was where people gathered to share the latest news. Nearby are remains of some graphite mines that were operated intermittently for more than a hundred years until 1978. Today the mine shafts are filled with water and fenced in.

Sunset glow over the harbor at Vinjesjøen.

HADSEL

Hadsel is a smaller island south of Langøy joined to the larger one by means of a stately bridge. On the north side there is Stokmarknes, in 1891 the birthplace of the famous coastal express. It is just as popular today and is something of a lifeline all along the coast from Bergen to Kirkenes. The Hurtigrute [coastal express] Museum, shows the development of transportation by sea in good times and bad. Roughly halfway between Storkmarknes and Melbu, on the south side of the island, lies the beautiful octagonal Hadsel Church. It is the latest in a succession of churches that have stood here. Hadsel Farm is mentioned already around the year 600 as the seat of a local king. The area around the church is indeed very rich in archaeological finds. The town of Melbu grew up around the turn of the century, thanks to one particular man, C. Frederiksen. In the course of a few years he turned the sleepy little trading post of some seventy residents in 1890 into a busy industrial town of a thousand people in 1920. Today the town is perhaps best known for its cultural festival, "Melbu in Summer," which attracts outstanding artists from home and abroad.

The bridge connecting Langøy to Hadsel is an elegant structure. An electric barrier on the bridge keeps the red fox from crossing over to Hadsel.

While grazing cows are not as common a sight in southern Norway, it is still the rule here. Hestneset, Hadsel.

On the west side of Hadsel the mountains drop steeply into the sea, as here at Hestneset. A hike along the ridge provides panoramic views of Lofoten and the ocean.

For many people, however, the mountains represent the great attraction. Hadsel is easily traversed end to end, a hike that takes you through green pastures and hills while you look down nine hundred feet onto the beach and skerries below, where the crystal-clear ocean rises and ebbs in its never-ending rhythm.

The cultural festival «Melbu in Summer» offers concerts, plays, markets, conferences, and much more to attract the crowds. The photo to the right is from a concert in the herring oil tank.

Previous page: In the winter the archipelago presents stark contrasts with snowy mountains and a leaden sea that never freezes. View from Hadsel towards Austvåg-øy.

HINNØYA – NORWAY'S LARGEST ISLAND

Hinnøya is Norway in miniature. This large island has rich farmland, extensive woods, long beaches, mountains to rival any range in Norway, as well as a city filled with historical treasures. You can spend a week on the island without having seen it all, and good roads make it easy to enjoy a variety of excursions in the area.

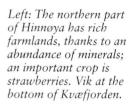

Mountain Hike in a Marine Setting

The Harstad Hiking Club has made a trail that has something for everyone. It starts in Harstad and heads south by way of three no-service huts, meaning you bring your own food, but the huts have the necessary housekeeping equipment. First the trail runs through easy lowlands, and then ascends onto the bare mountain with its spectacular views of sea and sound. It is almost like hiking in Jotunheimen, only here you have the ocean right next door. Along the way there are many lower peaks for those who like additional challenges.

Experienced hikers in good physical condition will appreciate a hike up Møysalen, the region's highest mountain. It probably earned the name, the Maiden's Saddle, because this is what it looks like from the south. Going without a guide is no problem, but most people join in on group hikes, all starting on the west side of the island, in the Lonkan Fjord. The hikes are organized by the Vesterålen Hiking

Left: The northern part of Hinnøya has rich farmlands, thanks to an abundance of minerals; an important crop is strawberries. Vik at the bottom of Kvæfjorden.

Below: Tjeldsund Bridge, the link between Hinnøya and the mainland, is among our largest and forms the entry gate to Lofoten and Vesterålen.

Trondenes Church north of Harstad is the region's only stone church and became important politically and culturally early on, as shown by numerous finds in and around the church.

Top right: "Greenland's apostle," Hans Egede, came from Hinnøya, and near the northern end of the island, by Elgsnes, a small chapel with an altar piece by Karl Erik Harr honors him.

Right: "Adolf," to the north of Trondenes Church, is the world's largest land cannon, with a range of thirty-five miles.

Club, so call the local tourist information office for information. Close to the top of the mountain a bit of climbing is required, but a metal chain has been bolted in place to assist you. If you prefer something steeper, with more drop-offs and bare rockfaces, there is plenty to choose from in the mountains to the west and north of Øksfjorden, with their sharp spires and knife-edges.

Trondenes Church – a Historical Landmark

The only stone church in Lofoten and Vesterålen, Trondenes Church just north of Harstad, is nicely situated right by the seashore. There is a weightiness in its solid, aspiring shape, and a wealth of Norwegian history, too. Trondenes was a cultural and political center for a very long time, also prior to the building of the church around 1250. At the time of the vikings Trondenes was the seat of a local king and the home of Asbjørn Selsbane, who was killed at Kabelvåg in 1020 under the orders of the Norwegian king Olaf

Haraldsson. At Alkevågen just north of the church there are archaeological sites revealing traces of large boathouses that may have held Asbjørn Selsbane's big viking ships. The church and adjacent museum buildings provide a good look at the history of the place.

You will even find recent history here. Just to the north of the church there is a somber reminder of the Second World War. The German Adolf cannon is the world's largest land cannon, and this one is centrally placed in a large bunker installation that shows its

development and use during the war. About sixty men were required for firing a single shot, so it is indeed huge. The cannon had a range of around thirty-five miles and could easily launch an attack on the harbor in Narvik!

From the church a path leads around Laugen Pond, known for its birdlife.

Harstad – City of Culture

Harstad also has other interesting sights. The city's cultural center has many kinds of events, and it is also the headquarters of the annual regional festival for northern Norway. If you have a car, you should take a drive to Elgsnes. Going over the mountain Aunfjellet, you will be rewarded with a terrific view. At Elgsnes there is a tiny chapel dedicated to Hans Egede, the "Apostle of Greenland," who came from here. The chapel is surrounded by archaeological sites and has an altarpiece decorated by the city's own Karl Erik Harr. The artist also has a print

gallery at Røkenes Manor and Restaurant. North of Harstad lie the islands Grytøy and Bjarkøy. The latter was home to the local king Tore Hund, known for his role in the killing of Olaf Haraldsson, at the Battle of Stiklestad. There are many other historical sites on

Top: Harstad is an important city in northern Norway, economically and culturally.

Above: Hemmestad by Gullesfjorden is a fishing plant turned local museum for the municipality of Kvæfjord.

*Grytøy is a striking,
mountainous island north
of Hinnøya, separated
from it by Toppsundet.*

Bjarkøy, and there is a detailed guide available.

Car Trip to Raftsundet

Raftsundet, the long sound separating Hinnøya from Austvågøy, has some of the wildest mountain terrain anywhere in Norway. Trollfjorden, which cuts into Austvågøy's western side, is well known, since the coastal express always stops there in the summer. It is also possible to see Raftsundet by car, and we can promise you a drive through surroundings you will long remember. Take road 822 to Kaljord by the Lonkan Fjord – which means this route can be combined with a visit to Møysalen – and take the ferry to Kongselv farther south. From Digermulen at the southern end of the sound you take a ferry across to Svolvær. If you want to see Raftsundet from the sea, there are boat trips from Svolvær.

AUSTVÅGØY

Lofoten Mountains

If you take the ferry across from Hadsel, glaciers and summits greet you on arrival, and words pale in this dramatic landscape. We recommend the somewhat longer and poorer road on the outside of the island, that is, you take an immediate right after leaving the ferry. The road winds into and out of fjords that have the finest sandy beaches and several good, strong tidal currents where the coalfish is eager to bite. The mountains line up all around you, reminding you of your insignificance in this landscape. You will need a generous supply of film for this place! When you return to the main road to Svolvær by Vestpollen, you have the proud profiles of Trolltinden and Higravtinden straight ahead.

Svolvær and Kabelvåg – the Heart of Lofoten

On the inside of Austvågøy, which has the richest fishing grounds in central Lofoten, lie Svolvær and Kabelvåg. The latter is located where King Eystein built a church already in 1103. At the time the place was called Vågan, a name which survives in that of the municipality. The king had fishermen's shanties put up for itinerant fishermen, an indication of the importance of the Lofoten Fishery at this early date. Kabelvåg was at one time the

Langstrandtind at the mouth of Raftsundet is one of many peaks that give the area its distinctly mountainous character.

Svolvær, the administrative center of Lofoten, is beautifully situated by the seashore with Jomfrutinden and Svolværgeita (next page) to the back.

Svolvær and Gallery Espolin in Kabelvåg show two genuine regional artists.

Svolværgeita [the Svolvær Goat], the steep twin peaks on the mountain to the back of the town, represents a cherished landmark in the area, with its two "horns." It takes both experience and climbing gear to make it to the top.

In Kabelvåg you will find the Lofoten Aquarium, a good place for getting acquainted with the creatures that live in the waters around here. Fishes in all shapes and colors, lobster, crab, and seals – they are all here, in a special building that has won a prize for its architectural quality. The Lofoten Museum with its presentation of local history is located virtually next door.

The Lofoten Cathedral in Kabelvåg is Lofoten's largest church, seating more than twelve hundred.

largest fishing village in Lofoten, but today Svolvær is the administrative center of the island. Visit the municipal center to have a look at Gunnar Berg's famous painting from the Battle of Trollfjorden, a legendary encounter between fishermen and steamboat owners.

Quite a few paintings can be seen in the area: Dagfinn Bakke's gallery in

Lofoten's only aquarium, near Kabelvåg, shows most species of marine life found in Lofoten and Vesterålen waters.

Henningsvær

This is a special fishing hamlet at the tip of Austvågøy. Houses built close together on small islands interconnected by bridges create an odd "urban" look with rows of warehouses bordering sounds and inlets. At the back of the hamlet Vågekallen rises, one of the best scenic lookouts in all of Lofoten and from the earliest times a familiar landmark to fishermen. The mountain is easily scaled from the back; you can also rent climbing gear or sign up for a local climbers' workshop. Karl Erik Harr has a gallery here, housing many of his paintings.

Svolværgeita, with its characteristic twin peaks towering above Svolvær, demands proper climbing gear if you want to get to the top.

Svolvær is one of many towns with a small market selling both vegetables and fish.

Fishing remains the most important source of income in the region. There are many big ocean-going fishing vessels, but some use small boats to supplement other income.

Although bridges and tunnels tie most of the region's islands together, there are still many ferries left, also those linking Lofoten to the mainland.

Skrova Lighthouse by Svolvær is strategically placed at Høla, important fishing grounds during the annual Lofoten

VESTVÅGØY – ISLAND OF THE VIKINGS

From Austvågøy there is a handsome bridge leading to Gimsøy, an island characterized by an unusual landscape. At one end of the island is a large bird sanctuary which includes the strange haystack-shaped mountain Hoven. A small bridge connects Gimsøy to Vestvågøy proper; and whether you drive on the inside by way of Stamsund or farther west through Borge, the

On Gimsøy Hoven rises like a pyramid from wetlands teeming with ducks and waders.

Contrasts are great in this mountain kingdom in the sea. The scene above is a summer dream, while in the photo on the right, taken only two months later, fall has set in with blustery weather at Leknes, the administrative center of Vestvågøy.

Left: Man is dwarfed against the Lofoten mountains. Sildpollnes at the bottom of Austfjorden, Austvågøy.

Youngsters here are as modern as anywhere else.

Gimsøy has Lofoten's only rune stone.

Elegant bridges link Gimsøy to neighboring islands, here the span from Austvågøy towards Gimsøy in the background.

Lofoten farming is often limited to a narrow strip of land with steep mountains to the back and the open sea in front. The rockslide to the back is a reminder that nature is always on the move.

Trout fishing is a favorite pastime for natives and visitors alike – here at Leknes.

roads meet in Leknes, the municipality's, as well as the island's, administrative center.

Lofotr Viking Museum

Large archaeological discoveries have been made in recent years at Borge, and they show that the vikings had an important seat out here. Today the main building has been recreated in its original form, measuring 240 by 18 feet, making it the largest of its kind in the Nordic countries. Inside there are exhibitions of artifacts found on the site, in addition to models showing everyday life as archaeologists imagine it to have been more than a thousand years ago. The style and size are impressive and bring us close to an age we know mostly through tales and legends. Down by the sea there is a boathouse in the original style, along with a large viking ship, a copy of the Gokstad ship,

now located at Bygdøy in Oslo. It was in these open ships that our forefathers traveled to Iceland, Greenland, and North America, and it is easy to see that a strong body and skilled seamanship were essential in an age that had none of our instruments and implements.

Eggum – Land of the Boulders

At Borge there is a side road leading westwards to Eggum. You are strongly advised to take it if you want a very special scenic experience. To the back of the houses at Eggum there is a large open meadow with a backdrop of vertical black rock walls. It is as if you are enjoying an orchestra seat in the midst of this grassy plain, watching the huge

The coastal express remains a lifeline even in an age of air traffic, and every stop, like this one at Stamsund, has one northbound and one southbound departure every day of the year.

Beautiful Unstad, on western Vestvågøy, is only one of the scenic spots awaiting you if you make an hour's detour.

Right: Eggum may well have Norway's finest boulder-strewn beach, with unusually large sea-polished stones.

Below right: The Nappstraum Tunnel between Vestvågøy and Flakstadøy has improved access, especially in winter snows and storms.

boulders on the beach. Nowhere else in Lofoten or Vesterålen will you find such large polished rocks. They show that the breakers have had an enormous power, and the result is a fantastic mosaic of shape and color. The odor of decomposing seaweed, the sound of the gulls, the beat of the waves, the hum of the wind, and the ocean's wide horizon before you combine to give you a symphony of scenic impressions. Only a "stony" person would be unmoved.

FLAKSTADØY

The Flakstad Trail –
a Walk through History

As you emerge from the subsea tunnel under Nappstraumen, park your car and start your walk several thousand years back in time. At Napp you find the trailhead for the Flakstad Trail, which runs all the way to Neslandsgårdene to the far south on the island. The hike takes several hours, but the physical exercise will pay off on this walk along a brim separating the sea and the mountains. After a while

Røssøystraumen Bridge ties communities on the west side of Selfjorden to the rest of Flakstad. Outer Moskenesøy also has some of the stateliest mountains in all of Lofoten.

you reach Storbåthallaren, one of Norway's most famous Stone Age sites. Sit down and imagine what life must have been like some six thousand years ago. The sea and the land were more abundant than they are now, and the people living here were resourceful. Cod, halibut, coalfish, and cusk featured on the menu, and the remains of twenty-seven different species of birds have been found, although gulls were naturally the most frequent dish. The islands were wooded back then, and occasionally reindeer, otter, deer, beaver, and seal also graced the stone table. What makes Storbåthallaren so special is the cave's dry interior; thanks to it, all organic materials have been preserved right up until our own time.

Leaving Storbåthallaren you continue down the path towards Nusfjord.

Nusfjord – a Photographer's Paradise
Nusfjord is among Norway's most frequently photographed scenic vistas. The tightly built fishing hamlet by the narrow harbor with a backdrop of steep mountains is totally irresistible to anyone in the possession of film and a camera. The buildings are well preserved and are kept painted in clear, bright colors. In case you want to spend a few days here, the place has many fishermen's shanties (but be sure to book months ahead if you are visiting in the summer); and in addition to the sea and fishing, the many scenic trails in the area provide ample hiking opportu-

Nusfjord – a photographers' favorite.

Sund is a tiny fishing hamlet near Sundstraumen at Flakstadøy. It has a metal sculpture smithy and shop and a small museum.

nities. A bit to the south of Nusfjord the old Nesland settlement still retains its original nineteenth-century form with separate buildings for everything: smokehouse, carpenter's workshop, mill, boathouse, barn, and so forth. Skjellfjorden, which you pass along the way, served as port of refuge during the Battle of Narvik in 1940. It has not always been as peaceful up here as it is now.

Selfjorden

The municipality of Flakstad encompasses not only Flakstadøy, but also the north end of Moskenesøy, along with Selfjorden and Sundstraumen, which separate the two islands. It is well worth making a stop here. Sundstraumen is one of Norway's most rapid tidal currents; it flows like a river through the narrow strait between high and low tide, and the fish really bite here. On the inside, Selfjorden lies sheltered by mighty rock walls to the west, but don't be intimidated. Drive across the bridge and on to Bergland. From here there is a good trail over the mountain to Kvalvika on the outside. The view from the top of the pass is truly remarkable. Below you lies the chalky white sand, which gradually turns green on entering the water, in front of you is the ever-vanishing horizon below the bright sky, while around you the mountains are lined up – spires, pinnacles, overhangs, rockfaces, pick your own terms, they are all here. This is a hike you are sure to rave about to anyone who wants to know where you spent your vacation.

Iron Cormorants

Just before crossing the bridge that joins Moskenesøy and Flakstadøy be sure to stop at Sund. It has a nice little smithy that turns out handsome works of art from "scrap" iron. The founder, Hans Gjertsen, became famous for his powerful and elegant cormorants made of iron; his successors also make other works of art. A small museum containing old machinery and tools is also worth a visit.

Selfjorden at Flakstadøy may be the most attractive fjord in all of Lofoten, surrounded by a multitude of peaks, pinnacles, and spires.

MOSKENESØY

Kirkefjorden and Reine
– Symbols of Lofoten

Moskenesøy is in a sense the end of Lofoten. Although Værøy and Røst lie still farther west, they seem mere specks in the sea compared to the enormous scale of the Lofoten Range.

The Range is great and dramatic, as if Geology and the Ice Age jointly decided to present their works. The mountains reach dizzying sweeps of three thousand feet from sea level to summit cairn, and scoured rockfaces, pointed crags, and sharp, airy knife-edges tie this alpine landscape together. For more than a hundred years painters and photographers have been flocking to this place. You can enjoy the best seats in the house if you drive across the bridges that skip lightly along at the far end of the fjord.

Barely across the last bridge and past a small bay you find yourself in Reine, a tiny, picturesque fishing hamlet that consists of beautiful and typical build-

Right: Thousands of visitors come to Lofoten and Vesterålen every year - to fish, to look, or, like our Polish friend, to seek inspiration.

Many people consider the fishing hamlet Reine the very essence of Lofoten's fjord and mountain landscape.

The fishing hamlet Hamnøy, located at the mouth of Kirkefjorden, faces the ocean and has the mountains to the back.

Stockfish retains its thousand-year tradition as a key export of the region. The cool, dry winter climate gives top quality.

Kirkefjord, at the bottom of Kirkefjorden, is among Lofoten's most secluded spots, reachable only by boat.

ings. Many of the region's fishing hamlets were earlier private enterprises, the property of a single local merchant /landowner, and some of them were only seasonally operated fishing stations. The Sverdrup family, who owned this one, have lived here for generations. Careful maintenance and beautiful surroundings make it another Lofoten showcase.

There are several fine mountain lakes, beautifully hidden away in the mountains around Reine and Sørvågen. The Lofoten Hiking Club has a very nice cabin up here, if you want to enjoy the midnight sun from the summits.

Refsvik – Outpost with a Gallery

Today there are no permanent residents on the ocean side of Moskenesøy, but up until the 1950s tiny dwellings were strung out along the area. They were established at a time when rowboats were still being used for fishing and when it was important to be close to the fishing grounds, so the people paid the price in a heavy assault from wind and sea. Today modern boats bring both the fishermen and others around to the outside, and it is a trip well worth your while. Once you have left Å, you can try your fishing luck farther out towards Lofotodden, a striking headland with narrow inlets and slippery reefs, but also with an idyllic little harbor beyond. You can go ashore and follow an attractive short trail over to Refsvik a bit to the north, and on your way down to the shore on the other side

Far left: The cave at Refsvik on Moskenesøy has many traces of earlier habitation, but is best known for its cave paintings.

Left: The paintings or drawings in the cave at Refsvik are among the few left from the Bronze Age.

Åvannet, near Å, where the Lofoten Road ends, has good fishing, and at the far end of the lake there is a trail leading across to the western side of the Lofoten Ridge.

Dried fish heads is a commodity saved for later grinding into animal feed.

you will find Refsvikhulen. For security reasons this visit has to be guided, because three-thousand-year-old cave paintings are not common in Norway.

If you are really spry, you will walk back to Å, although it is not recommended on a stormy day. Then you take the boat back to Å. If you are in the mood for more, stop by the Norwegian Stockfish Museum and the Norwegian Fishing Station Museum to get an impression of earlier ways of life.

Å has more than 100,000 visitors a year, many of them school children on excursion.

At Å you find the world's only stockfish museum, which shows advances in products and tools through a thousand years.

Practice makes perfect. This budding young fisherman has gotten a head start on his apprenticeship.

Between the islands Mosken and Lofotodden in the background is where we find the famous Moskenes Current, or Maelstrom, one of the world's strongest tidal currents.

Lofotodden is very exposed, open to winds from all sides. Stormy weather can come suddenly rolling in from the ocean.

VÆRØY

Like Røst, Værøy is an outpost in the ocean. The island is shaped like a massive curved rock wall to the west and the ocean, effectively sheltering a wide flat beach on the opposite side. This was where people settled, and this is where we find all the houses, the school, the church, and the ferry landing. All roads, a total of thirteen miles, have their starting point here. As in the rest of the Lofoten municipalities, fishing is their means of survival along with summer tourism. Værøy is optimally situated near the large fishing grounds, and productivity is very high. Stockfish for the Italian market is the main product.

The mountain ridge to the west is easy to climb from the inside, both by footpath and on a gravel road that leads up to a telecommunications and radio station located on top of Heia, the tallest mountain on the island. The trip is highly recommended; the view up here is magnificent: the expanse of the ocean to the west, Lofotodden and the peaks on Moskenesøy to the north, and the Narvik mountains to the east, with the great glacier, Svartisen, to the far southeast.

The houses at Værøy lie sheltered on a wide shore on the lee side of a broad mountain ridge.

Værøy is a special outpost in the ocean; abundant year-round fishing provides a living for a surprising number of people out here.

There are many weather-beaten houses in Lofoten. Some are now used only in summer.

The Lundehund

Like the inhabitants of Røst, the people at Værøy derived part of their livelihood from bird catching, and puffins constituted their most important catch. The birds were caught by the aid of a net thrown off the top of the bird cliffs to entrap them. At Værøy, however, the Lundehund [puffin dog] was also used for the hunt. This is a native Norwegian breed of dog whose origin is unknown, but stone-age finds dating back five thousand years indicate that it is very old. The dog is a so-called spitz, and its special traits are its small size and agility, which enable it to crawl into the puffins' subterraneous nests and pull out adult birds. It is anatomically unique and differs from all other dog breeds in having an extra toe but lacking a molar. The Lundehund is also able to physically shut its ears, a useful skill when crawling through the narrow underground passages. An unusual flexibility of the neck and well-anchored ligaments in the shoulder joints make it especially well suited for subterraneous hunting.

This kind of hunt now belongs to the

past. During the Second World War the breed came close to extinction when the few remaining dogs developed distemper. The breed survived only because there were a few dogs elsewhere, and today there are about six hundred of them.

Mostadgrenda – Home of the Norwegian Lundehund

From Nordlandet a good path runs along the seaward side of the island, and you just have not seen Værøy if you haven't taken this route over Eidet to Mostad on the opposite side. It is a memorable experience, both visually and aurally, to stand there with the mountains at your back, the ocean in front, and everything draped in lush and colorful vegetation and alive with the most ear-shattering cacophony of feathered residents. Mostad is today uninhabited, but its soul lives on between the vertical rock wall and the

narrow shoreline in front of it. This was the home of the Norwegian Lundehund before the entire breed was nearly wiped out.

On the outside of the Mostad peninsula lie Værøy's largest bird cliffs. For those in good physical condition it is no problem getting to the top, but great caution is needed just on top of the bird cliffs. The ground is treacherous, con-

The Norwegian Lundehund was earlier used for underground puffin hunting. The dog crawled in and pulled the birds out from their burrows. Stone Age finds show that the breed is very old.

In fair weather photo subjects abound.

Right: Modern fishing vessels have the latest equipment, in communication, navigation, and for bringing in the catch.

cealing numerous puffin burrows, it is always windy up here, and in rainy weather it is slippery. Many people have fallen off in their eagerness to see more of the cliffs than can be seen from the edge. Instead you are advised to join one of the daily boat trips to the bird colonies. You will get more out of that than a trip on your own, mostly because the boats have local guides who are familiar with the peculiarities of both the birds and their habitats.

In case you prefer not to walk back from the Mostad area, you can arrange to be picked up by boat. On the way back you stop by at Stranden, one of Norway's most unusual beaches. On the south side of Heia, nature has prepared a wonderful, completely sheltered beach, facing south and protected by an almost twelve-hundred-foot vertical rock wall. On sunny days it can get so hot here that it feels more like a stay at the Riviera than a visit above the Arctic Circle. The only access to Stranden is by boat, unless you are a bona fide mountain climber.

Eagle Hunting

There are few places in Norway where you will see as many gray sea eagles as at Værøy. Every year several pairs nest

Fishing on the warf is a favorite pastime of boys at any age. Here billets provide the catch.

Below: Wherever you turn in Lofoten and Vesterålen there are views to be captured and brought back home to lure new travelers to the islands.

Right: There are few places in the world where you can see as many gray sea eagles. Young birds may take five years to find a mate and stake a territory.

out here, and flocks of young ones are frequently seen circling above the bird colonies in search of prey.

Previously the eagles were caught because they represented a threat to sheep farming by directly attacking the lambs or chasing them over a cliff. At Værøy hunters developed their own technique, building small stone huts for the hunter to hide in near the top of the cliffs. Bait was put out on the roof of the hut; and when the eagle landed, the hunter grabbed it by the legs through a small hatch, and the eagle had no chance of escape. Today all eagles are protected by Norwegian law, and the hunt is a thing of the past.

Overleaf: The great whirlpool of the Moskenes Current makes it an excellent fishing spot for gulls and other birds. Here we see kittiwakes at rest while the tide turns. Mosken, in the background, is also known for its large gannet colony.

The Maelstrom

Between Værøy and Lofotodden lies the islet Mosken. It is uninhabited and all around it run some of the world's strongest tidal currents. The wide tidal range in Lofoten and the frequent long periods of strong winds combine to make the current very strong and dangerous to small boats. Already in the fifteenth century Bishop Olaus Magnus, who had not personally experienced the current, describes it, clearly exaggerating its force and size. Myths spread fast, and in 1591 the local tax official Schønnebøl reports that the current at times is so strong that the locks fall out of the doors in neighboring islands. The dead whales that occasionally drift ashore in Lofoten and Vesterålen were

Stockfish is one of Vær-øy's most important exports.

thought to have been killed in the current. In the world-famous novel *Twenty Thousand Leagues Under the Sea* Jules Verne uses the Moskenes Current by having Captain Nemo and his submarine Nautilus disappear into the bowels of the earth in it.

Exaggeration aside, the Moskenes Current is well worth a visit – in a proper vessel. The current is very powerful and irregular; at its strongest it is like sitting in the middle of an enormous flood. Large whirlpools swiftly appear and disappear, and together with the roar of the seething waters it is almost magical when you look at the calm waters on both sides of the sound.

RØST

Røst is a fairyland in the sea – totally different from the rest of Lofoten and Vesterålen. Hundreds of large and small islands are strewn everywhere with their narrow bays and inlets where the tide rushes forth and falls back in its never-ending daily rhythm. The smell of seaweed and salt water stays with you, along with the calls of the ever-present gulls hovering above, while somber eiders bob along the shoreline. There is a grandeur and a freshness in this landscape rarely seen elsewhere in Norway. The sky is wide and fades into the ocean's long horizon both on clear summer days and at times when white-topped breakers wash ashore. The long lines of Værøy and Moskenesøy are broken only by facing the end of the Lofoten Range.

Røstlandet, the main island in the group, is as flat as a dance floor, the highest point reaching a mere thirty-three feet above sea level. It is here on the landward side of the islands that people settled, and this is home to seven hundred residents, making Røst one of Norway's tiniest municipalities. Hundreds of white houses are scattered about, surrounded by small patches in the form of fields, pastures, ponds, and numerous inlets and brackish pools. Along the inlets on the leeward side you find all the fish processing plants, the tangible evidence of Røst's most important industry, the

Nearly every visitor to Røst arrives by ferry, from either Bodø or Moskenesøy via Værøy.

The bird cliffs at Røst
are world famous, for
their size as well as their
diversity of species.
Each year many foreign
ornithologists also come
to study the area's bird
life.

     RØST

fisheries. Here all the fish is processed: salted, fileted, or dried on racks; the latter practice leaves its imprint on the landscape near the houses. The combination of mild winters and cool summers produces excellent stockfish, exported primarily to southern Europe. Around the clock throughout the year vessels come and go through the sounds and narrow inlets, the screech of winches matching those of the shrill kittiwakes that make their homes on the colorful warehouses. Added to the crystal-clear, cold water, the rocking brown seaweeds, the numerous gulls on the warehouses and the ever-present smell of fish give this harbor by the great ocean a very special ambience.

Surrounding Røstlandet, with its airstrip and ferry landing, there are hundreds of islets, most of them uninhabited. Aside from gulls and other birds, the only creatures are sheep, and most of them roam free year-round because of the mild climate. In fact Røst can boast Norway's highest average temperature during the winter, despite the sun's absence for fifty days during the winter season. It is right in the path of the Gulf Stream, which brings warm water all the way from the Gulf of Mexico.

Røst has been inhabited since about B.C. 2000, but there is ample evidence that these islands were abandoned during times of poor fishing and resettled when the fish returned. The dearth of wood for heating and building material may have been a contributory factor in this periodic pattern of habitation. For

Røstlandet is surrounded by islands that have some of Norway's largest bird colonies. From left: Hærnyken, Trenyken, Ellevsnyken, and Storfjellet. To the far left: Skomvær, the end of Lofoten.

instance Storøya has had settlements
that must have depended largely on
fowling for their livelihood. If the idea
of spending some hours or days on a
deserted island appeals to you, hire a
boat and bring your tent and sleeping
bag. Driftwood can be found along the
beach, and there is plenty of fish and
fresh air; the latter keeps arriving in
ample measure from the ocean, so don't
forget your windbreaker.

The Bird Cliffs

To the west of the level Røstlandet there
is a monumental lineup of precipitous
islands: Vedøy, Storfjellet, Ellefsnyken,
Trenyken, and Hernyken. On these we
find Norway's largest bird colonies.
The puffins predominate in the steep
grassy areas, while guillemots, kittiwakes, and razorbills prefer the vertical

rock walls down towards the water.
There are many other species, such as
cormorants, black guillemots, various
species of gulls, Arctic petrels, and the
rare stormy petrels, which arrive in the
breeding colonies only when darkness
descends upon the land once more. All
this has made Røst one of the better-
known bird habitats in northern
Europe.

A visit to these bird colonies is
something you will long remember,
whether you stay onboard or go
ashore. The air next to the cliffs is full
of birds leaving for their hunting
grounds or returning, and the noise is
deafening. There is teeming life not just
on the rocky cliffs, but also on the sea,
covered by birds in the thousands, as
little black and white specks in con-
stant search of food. Time of day and

night plays no part in this inexorable forward movement of life itself; and above it all hover the raven and the eagle, ready to descend on anyone showing signs of weakness or falling off the edge. Along the foot of the mountain scurvy grass and sorrel form dense, lush meadows, fertilized by all the bird droppings from the cliffs above.

In times past fowling was a vital nutritional and financial resource for the people of Røst. Especially young puffins and cormorants were gathered, along with an enormous number of eggs. During the Second World War as many as 200,000 salted puffins were shipped off from Røst annually. The hunting was done by the use of a net spread out over the roosting field, entrapping the puffins as they emerged from their burrows. This hunt is now

illegal, but it still takes place to a lesser extent under the pretext of age-old cultural traditions. The eggs used to be stored in darkness in dry sand, and under these conditions they kept for months.

Skomvær

Skomvær is the very outermost point of Lofoten, and already in 1887 a large lighthouse was built here for the benefit of all the fishing boats that frequented the area, especially in the winter. Today the lighthouse has been automated and left uninhabited.

The sister of the illustrator Theodor Kittelsen was married to the keeper of the lighthouse at Skomvær, and Kittelsen lived with them for a couple of years. This resulted in a number of beautiful drawings of birds and scenery

Summer is the time for boat maintenance and care, after rough treatment suffered through another stormy winter season on the frequently turbulent sea.

Skomvær Lighthouse is Lofoten's end point and one of the most exposed and weatherbeaten spots in all of Norway. The artist Theodor Kittelsen spent two years here when his brother-in-law was the lighthouse keeper, but today it has been automated and abandoned.

and also his famous illustrations of the legend of Utrøst.

Utrøst was supposed to be a place of exceptionally good fishing grounds beyond the lighthouse at Skomvær. Many legends refer to these grounds, which were reputed to give a home to the legendary figure *draugen*, frequently pictured as a semi-human creature representing the ghost of someone lost at sea. The Norwegian fairytale collector Asbjørnsen recorded much of this tradition in his tale "Skarvene på Utrøst" [The Cormorants at Utrøst]. Fish that had grain in their guts or straw in the gills were said to have visited the underwater kingdom of *draugen* and helped themselves to his grainfields.

An Italian at Røst

In April 1431 an Italian merchant, Pietro Querini, left Crete on a large ship with a cargo of wine and a crew of sixty-eight for Brugge, Belgium. In the dark of night on January 6, 1432, following an eventful voyage that included several shipwrecks, they managed to get ashore on one of the smaller Røst islands. Some died from fatigue and exposure, but a few weeks later the survivors were found by a fisherman. The local minister knew Latin, so the unfortunate visitors were able to communicate, even here at the far ends of Europe. It was May 14 before they could head south again. There are two written accounts of this remarkable trip. One was recorded by Querini himself, the other by a scribe, based on talks and interviews with the rest of the crew. These records give us a very detailed picture of the everyday life of ordinary people such a long time ago.

Anyone interested in Norwegian history ought to read Querini's account. It has recently (1991) been included, in a new Norwegian translation, in a book inspired by Querini's voyage written by H.A. Wold, *I paradisets første krets* [In the First Circle of Paradise]. At Sandøy, where the Italians are said to have landed, a granite marker has been erected to commemorate this strange incident.

MOUNTAINS AND ROCKS

The most striking feature of the Lofoten and Vesterålen landscape is the contrast between the typically level shore and the precipitous mountains in the background.

The width of the shore ranges all the way from a narrow strip of land to which a few houses cling tenaciously to wide, rolling farmland as we find it on Vestvågøy and at Langøy on the western side of Vesterålen. The land levels out from the steep mountains in the background towards the shoreline and in many places beyond it, to a varied archipelago and to the fishing reefs farther out. Finally there is "the edge," the continental margin, which drops off into the great ocean deep.

It is the sea that has chiselled this coastline in the course of millennia. Through the ages wave upon wave has broken up the rocks, ground them into gravel and sand and pulled this material seaward. In some places it was lost in the deep, in others it was deposited on the bottom. When the land subsequently rose or the sea receded, these flat areas dried out, and today they form the basis of rich agricultural acreage.

Sea and land have altered their level through these millions of years. During ice ages the great mass of ice pushed the area down dozens of feet. At the same time there was so much ice covering land worldwide that during the last ice age the sea level was 360 feet below current levels. This meant that Lofoten and Vesterålen formed a continuous land mass with a wide tundra sloping towards the brink of the continental margin. When the ice disappeared, the land began to rise because the pressure of this weight was gone. At the same time the sea rose, due to melting water, and began scratching and washing away the former tundra. Waves and currents carried sand, clay, and gravel into sheltered spots and coves. Reefs and low rocks were washed clean, and stones and rocks along the foot of the mountains were gradually polished into smooth and pretty pebbles and boulders.

This has taken millions of years. Just now land and sea have arrived at a seeming equilibrium, and we see a coastline of green fields, wide moors, and a peaceful archipelago. Every now and again, however, you might let your mind wander back to that distant era as you move along the shore, because that is the time you experience most keenly when visiting Lofoten and Vesterålen.

The rock formations generally fall into two categories. One consists of a

Lofoten rock is mostly hard and has withstood the ravages of time fairly well, as in Vågekallen, Austvågøy, a Lofoten landmark.

Following the Ice Age and prior to growth of vegetation, the wind raged freely through the large quantities of loose material deposited. The picture shows an old sand dune the wind is gradually grinding down, exposing the fine structure. Each storm left a thin layer, sometimes only sand, at other times mixed with fine, brown soil particles.

Nowhere in Lofoten is the region's alpine character as evident as in the mountains along Kirkefjorden beyond Reine, Moskenesøy. These mountains consist of gneiss, a rock very resistant to the harsh, destructive effects of external forces.

worn-down plane that rose before erosion started its destructive work. In these mountain areas you usually walk on a fairly level plain that drops off steeply towards the sea. The remains of such a plateau are clearly in evidence on Værøy and parts of Hinnøya and Grytøy.

The other type of formation is younger and gives the mountains a far

The shores of Lofoten and Vesterålen have been formed by ice and the sea through millions of years. In exposed places, such as Varberg, Flakstadøy, winter storms have washed the rock clean, followed by ice and frost, which have left their traces on the surface. On the peninsula in the background the old peneplain is clearly noticeable.

more alpine appearance with jagged peaks, narrow ridges and sloping drop-offs. You find such mountains in Moskenesøy and Flakstadøy and in the area around Raftsundet. In both cases the ice continued its grinding and scouring through all of the four ice ages we have had during the most recent millennia. This led to a displacement of the deposited material: small lakes were formed and bowls and u-shaped valleys dug out all over the area.

The bulk of the Lofoten-Vesterålen archipelago consists of ancient and very hard metamorphic rocks of predominantly gneiss, granite, and syenite. Only the northern part of Hinnøya has softer, sedimentary rocks that crumble easily, giving the entire area a soft appearance. At Andøya we find some of the youngest rock in Norway, formed during the Cretaceous period approximately 120 million years ago. This is also where we find the only coal-fields in Norway proper. See Andøya chapter for further details.

Overleaf: A glacier grinds approximately one milli-meter (0.04 inch) off the rock below it per year, and in sheltered, shallow areas much of this silt can be found in fine sandy or sand-filled boulder beaches, as here at Værøy.

SKIES AND SEAS

This is north of the Arctic Circle, so there is midnight sun in the summer. We are not far north of the Circle, but Røst has midnight sun for nearly fifty nights, while Andøya farther north has an additional ten days. If you want to catch the midnight sun here, you have to visit between May 20 and July 23. Prior to and following these dates it is still light all night, because the sun dips only slightly below the horizon in its brief daily nap.

However, what you and local residents enjoy in summer is not present in winter. If you return then, you will find the sun gone almost as long as you previously enjoyed the midnight sun. There is not total darkness, for the snow brightens things up, and when the weather is clear, the stars and the moon throw a pale and enchanting nocturnal light over the white mountains and the dark sea. Some years there are also northern lights illuminating the sky with their flickering yellowish-green light, giving you a memorable visual experience. So treat yourself to a winter visit, as well. It will be something totally different.

If you come to Lofoten and Vesterålen for a suntan, you have really missed the mark. This is, after all, far up north, and the summers are on the cool side, no two ways about it. There are many sunny days, but you must come prepared for some windy days with rain or drizzle even in July and August. It is, after all, the rapid changes that make the area special, and this applies to weather as well as the landscape. So bring warm clothes and savor the strong gusts and the clean air with its pungent aroma of salt and seaweed.

There is midnight sun fifty to sixty days a year in the region, and the unusual angle of light always creates a special atmosphere.

In places sheltered from the waves there are often extensive shoreland flats, full of birds, fish, and small animals.

Next page: The archipelago's great tidal range leaves large exposed areas of shiny seaweed tangles at ebb tide, allowing the numerous birds to help themselves to the rich fauna that thrives in this environment.

The Gulf Stream with its warm currents continuously flows alongside the many islands and reefs of Lofoten and Vesterålen; but we are far removed from the Mexican Gulf, and the water temperature rarely exceeds ten or twelve degrees centigrade in the summer, except in sheltered coves.

Tidal highs and lows are caused by the power of attraction exerted on the earth by the sun and the moon, and thanks to the area's geographic placement, it has some of Norway's greatest differences in sea level, often reaching a tidal range of some nine feet. This creates strong tidal currents when narrow bays and inlets are to be emptied or filled every six hours. One result is

good fishing, but it can create problems for boaters, especially when boats are tied up. It also demands alertness if you do your own boating out here. The channel you passed through with ease a few hours ago may be dried up on your return. The wide tidal range also alters the coastal landscape, because at ebb tide the sea may recede several hundred yards and expose large littoral areas. It is well worth exploring these big exposed flats. There is often teeming marine life among the stones and seaweed, crabs, sea urchins, snails, starfish, and other creatures.

FLORA

Lofoten's varied landscape, ranging from wide open beaches through bogs and moors to Hinnøya's lofty peaks, makes for a very rich plant life. Habitats alter quickly from sandy beaches to arid moors harboring dryland plants and on to lakes and ponds with typical wetland vegetation and rich forests and cold-loving plants near snow patches. A host of cultivars, among them some persistent weeds, have accompanied human beings into the area.

One characteristic of the Lofoten and Vesterålen flora is the presence of plants that in southern Norway would be part of the mountain flora. Plants like mountain avens and purple saxifrage are found right down to the water's edge alongside sea pink and sea sandwort. This is due to the cool summers that allow high altitude plants to survive life at sea level without drying out.

There is no complete guide to all the species found in Lofoten and Vesterålen, so you have to make use of standard plant guides or reference works if you want the names of them

Left: All along the shoreline, even in the most exposed places, you find the sea pink. Its tolerance of saltwater spray often leaves it no competition on the outermost rocky shore.

What makes the region's plant life special is the mix of seashore and alpine flora. The campion shown here thrives all the way down to the seashore.

The mountain birch is making a comeback after near extinction during times when wood was in greater demand. Wind and snow twist the trees; only those sheltered have straight trunks.

all. The following section will give you a survey and a more detailed description of some of the most typical plants found throughout the islands.

Vegetation

Traveling from the mainland, you will soon discover that these islands are for the most part unforested. On the western side extensive salt spray keeps the forest down, but the absence of trees in Lofoten and Vesterålen is above all the work of man. Widespread use of wood stoves in winter, use of wood as building material, along with the persistent grazing of pastureland took a heavy toll on the forest. A lot of wood was used

for making racks for the preservation of fish. Cod-liver oil production also consumed a considerable quantity of wood. In the nineteenth century all this left the land nearly unforested. However, thanks to electric power and fewer domestic animals on pasture, the birch woods are now reappearing all over the islands. In another hundred years they will be wooded once more, the way they were before the arrival of man.

The relatively high rate of precipitation and the cool summers allow rapid development of bogs in poorly drained level areas. Lofoten and Vesterålen therefore have vast wetlands. Many of these have been drained and cultivated, but the largest flats remain, especially at Andøya, where we find some of the most extensive bogs in Norway. The bogs were used for pasture and for cloud-berry picking, but when the forest disappeared, they were also harvested as fuel in the form of peat.

Cloudberries

These golden, sweet, juicy, and rather seedy fruits are a Norwegian institution, widely regarded as a great delicacy. If you are served this as a dessert treat, you would do well to appreciate the sweet flavor and overlook the gritty texture.

Cloudberries are found on all peat bogs in Lofoten and Vesterålen, and every fall local residents eagerly harvest the berries. Andøya has some of the best cloudberry bogs, and their harvesting has long been an important source of income for local residents. Cloudberries, unlike other berries growing on uncultivated land, cannot be freely picked. The law stipulates that cloudberries growing in our three northernmost counties are the property of the landowner, precisely because of their high price and their value to the local population. If you are planning to go cloudberry-picking at Andøya, for instance, you need permission from the local law enforcement. This is fairly routine towards the end of the season, because the bogs are enormous, so there is usually enough for everyone.

What has made Andøya into a cloudberry-pickers' eldorado is, of course, the extensive bogs, but also the mild climate. Cloudberries are arctic alpine plants that are not found to the south on the European continent. Nonetheless the plant is very vulnerable

Left: Cloudberries are common in Lofoten and Vesterålen and provide a profitable sideline for the local population. The mild coastal climate prevents freezing, a frequent hazard in the mountains.

The cloudberry is the exclusive property of the landowner, and you will often see signs prohibiting the picking of these berries. Other berries can be picked freely.

to frost at all stages of flowering. A few minutes of freezing temperatures, either during flowering or ripening, will spoil the entire harvest. In the mountains of Norway there are often a few hours of frost some time during the summer, for example on clear nights following rain, and this ruins the cloudberry harvest for that area.

Lofoten and Vesterålen never have frost during the summer, so the berries are not damaged by freezing temperatures. There are still, however, good and bad years for cloudberries, and the reason is the weather during flowering. The cloudberry plant is unisexual, so don't be fooled by a snow-white bog in spring. There may be a preponderance of "male" plants, but these do not produce berries. The cloudberry flower is wide open and is thus susceptible to bad weather, which is fairly frequent in Andøya's level terrain. A cold and blustery May can destroy the entire harvest since insects are inactive in cold, damp weather, and the flowers are filled with water or get blown to pieces.

Human beings are not alone in regarding cloudberries as a delicacy; the birds do, too, especially the thrushes, and they do a good job of scattering the seeds. In situ cloudberries spread effectively by means of runners; and if conditions are favorable, they may form a carpet of offshoots all originating in one plant. This is a reason for the phenomenon of one area having nothing but "male" plants, while a few yards away there is a whole moundful of golden berries on "female" plants.

Cloudberries are tolerant of the acid peat but have little ability to compete in better soil, so the cloudberry is pretty well confined to peat bogs.

What made and makes the cloudberry one of our most valuable berries, is the high content of vitamin C. Of course, our ancestors did not know what vitamins were, but they quickly realized that cloudberries were effective in warding off the dreaded ailment scurvy. The cause of this illness was in fact vitamin C deficiency, and it was widespread among sailors and people

The marsh marigold brightens streams and edges of ponds; its seeds float easily and spread in such areas. The plant is poisonous and ignored by grazing animals.

Cottongrass is pretty and easy to spot and grows all over Norway. The "cotton" is the hair growing on the seeds, helping to spread them.

in the north, where the supply of fruit and vegetables used to be very poor. In addition to a high vitamin C content cloudberries (and lingonberries, for that matter) contain a lot of benzoic acid, nature's very own preservative. It keeps mold and bacteria away, so cloudberries can be stored unprocessed, unlike other berries, which had to be dried before sugar and freezers became readily available.

Scurvy grass

Scurvy grass belongs to the cabbage family and is generally found along the seashore. It has small, white flowers with four petals and small, round silicles, or capsules. In some locations the plants are fairly insubstantial, but in well-fertilized places, as for instance those found below bird cliffs or on large beached tangles of seaweed, they can grow into a vigorous green mesh. The leaves are thick and fleshy, enabling the plant to conserve water, a commodity that, oddly enough, is in short supply on the seashore. For the plants cannot make use of salt water, and sand and gravel are incapable of retaining the rainwater no matter how it pours. Throughout history people living along the coast have used scurvy grass as a source of vitamin C. Scurvy was a much feared disease in earlier times, but our ancestors found that cloudberries and scurvy grass kept this affliction at bay. The nineteen-century writer Lilienskiold describes it like this: "In this country the herb is carefully gathered as winter cabbage and for other use, and it is among the most effective preventives in the nation's defense against the harsh assaults of scurvy." Scurvy grass was usually preserved in a mild brine to keep it fresh and palatable.

Left: Scurvy grass used to be harvested in the fight against scurvy, an illness caused by vitamin C deficiency now hardly known in Norway.

Already in the Middle Ages angelica archangelica was grown as a vegetable and a medicinal herb.

Angelica

Angelica archangelica, or garden angelica, is a large, green umbelliferous plant growing in both damp alpine soils and along the shore. The latter is referred to as "shore angelica" and differs from the alpine variety. Both grow in Lofoten and Vesterålen and were previously often used as vegetables. Already at the time of the vikings angelica had a wide reputation as a healing remedy, in addition to its role as a vegetable. The plant is mentioned already in the Norse poet and historian Snorri Sturluson's saga of King Olaf Tryggvason, whose attempts to introduce Christianity and subdue the local kings ended with the Battle of Svolder in 1000. Following the arrival of Christianity in Norway, monks carried the plant back to the European continent. This may be Norway's sole contribution to the world's supply of vegetables. Angelica was thought especially effective against the plague, which it is not, and the plant is no longer being used, not even in this country. However, at the time Linné was so impressed by its qualities that in 1753 he named it Angelica archangelica. This actually doubles the angels, because "Angelica" means angel, and for extra measure he added the arch angel.

Tromsø Palm

A late arrival in Lofoten and Vesterålen is what is nationally known as the Tromsø palm. It is a giant umbelliferae, a cow parsnip or giant hogweed by the Latin name *Heracleum laciniatum*, which has yellow-green flowers forming broad, curved clusters. The history of the plant remains unclear, but it seems to have arrived originally in England from Asia. Around 1850 seeds were sent from there to the mining community Kåfjord in Alta, where English mining engineers were employed at the time. The plant found conditions in Alta a bit too arid, but once seeds were shipped to Tromsø, it quickly took hold. In no time it spread to the entire island of Tromsøy and was dubbed the Tromsø "palm," thanks to its size and wide umbels. Today the plant is found all over northern Norway, and it, or related species, have started popping up in southern parts as well.

The problem with the Tromsø palms is that they are nearly impossible to get

"Tromsø palm" earned the name for its size and its profusion in that area. It is mildly poisonous and shunned by animals. Although its origin is unknown, its current familiarity is constantly spreading.

rid of, and they overtake everything else. Once they enter a fairly soggy pasture, these six to nine foot tall plants soon invade the entire field. Like many other umbelliferae they are mildly poisonous, and the animals will not eat them. Many people develop a rash after touching the plant, so this is a troublesome, if decorative, foreigner.

Oyster Plant

The oyster plant, or lungwort, will settle for the most barren of soils. Far out on a coarse, rocky shore or among large boulders it finds shelter and anchorage. The plant creeps along the ground, and in favored spots it can form pretty little mats of blue flowers and shiny bluish-green foliage. The leaves are juicy, good at water retention – fresh water is always in short supply on the seashore. Evaporation is reduced through a thin wax coating on the leaves, which also causes the faintly bluish-green color.

The unmistakable hint of oyster in the salty flavor of the leaves has given name to the plant, which indeed has served as a vegetable in times of scarcity along the coast.

Sea Rocket

On every sandy beach in Lofoten and Vesterålen you will find the sea rocket, with its characteristic pinkish purple petals and disjointed stems growing in tangles on the sand. It is nearly unrivalled in tolerating such exposed sites, where water is scant, and wind and grains of sand can make life rather difficult. The fruit is actually a capsule or a *silicula*, as it is referred to in the cabbage family, where the sea rocket belongs, but the capsule looks like a tiny arrowhead and contains one seed.

Seaweed

Walking along sounds and inlets you cannot miss what is possibly the lushest and most impressive flora in the region, namely the extensive "forests" of kelp and rockweeds. Nearly everywhere

Red campion is found in meadows and along roads, and also on deep woodland soil.

Left: Oyster plant thrives on coarse sand and rocks by the seashore. The thick leaves tolerate drought and saltwater spray, leaving it almost unchallenged along the beach.

Mountain avens is a good example of how alpine flora can also be found at lower elevation in the Lo-foten-Vesterålen archipel-ago; given a bit of alkalinity, it will thrive down to the water's edge.

The tufted saxifrage stays mostly in the mountains farther south, but due to the cool summers it readily makes its way to the seashore here in the north.

below the surface of the sea they cling tenaciously to the rock, and in the clear water they sway to the rhythm of the tide.

You will soon notice the considerable difference between ebb and high tide, which in many places lays bare large mud flats and rocky coves. The algae that are to survive in this environment must be able to tolerate a few hours of drying in the sun on a hot summer day or the sharp cold snap on a dark and chilly winter night. Through millions of years species have emerged that are tolerant of such treatment, and especially common in such an environment is the brown bladder wrack that floats on the surface, where it receives maximum light, by means of its large air bladders. On stones and cliffs you will find the much shorter "sheep wrack," so-called because the sheep graze on it when they crave salt.

Along shorelines least exposed to

Seaweeds are especially abundant in Lofoten and Vesterålen, and each species finds its place in the ecosystem depending on its tolerance for being dried out or torn by the breakers. Large quantities are harvested for use in the production of alginates.

wave action, where fresh and salt water alternate, there is often a thin layer of green algae. They are too fragile to survive exposure to stronger waves and currents.

The brown bladder wrack and fellow species prefer inlets and channels with a swift flow of water but without strong waves and currents. On skerries and smooth rocky shores facing the open sea we find the large brown sweet tangle with its yardlong flat and pliable "leaves." They are attached to cliffs and boulders by means of a powerful stipe widened at the base; and the grip is so strong that the average man will fail in attempts to dislodge it. Also, their pliability lets them simply move with the water, lessening its impact. In addition they normally form dense "forests," which allows individual plants to contribute to and benefit from the protection of the community. Dense seaweed colonies naturally provide favorable habitats for a variety of animals and fishes. Spend a few minutes by a ferry quay or on a seaside rock and watch the fascinating life unfolding in these underwater forests. The entire "forest" itself will be seen to perform a slow-motion ballet of ever-changing, fluid movements choreographed by currents and swells.

Undoubtedly our ancestors also appreciated the beauty of seaweeds, but they also harvested them as food for horses and cattle when the winter supply of hay was low. They also used seaweeds as fertilizer, since all rockweeds are high in important minerals. Today seaweeds no longer serve these functions, but thousands of tons are now cut for the production of the alginates that we find in toothpaste, creams, low-calorie frostings, and ice creams.

BIRDS

Nowhere else in Norway will you see the rich birdlife found in Lofoten and Vesterålen. Each year the area is visited by professional ornithologists from all over Europe, along with many amateur bird watchers pursuing their hobby under close to ideal conditions. The open landscape makes it easy to observe the birds, and most of them are relatively confiding and approachable.

Whether you are a bird watcher or some other kind of traveler, your visit will be considerably more rewarding if you bring along a pair of binoculars and a handy bird guide. Wherever you go out here you'll be surrounded by birds – in the air and on the water, not only individuals, but flocks numbering thousands of gulls on the skerries and birds by the million on the cliffs.

The reason for this varied and abundant birdlife is twofold. In the first place, the close proximity of different habitats. Within a range of a few hundred yards you move from skerries and bird cliffs to sheltered brackish pools and small ponds harboring waders and ducks. Farther inland there are moors and birch forests sheltering their typical species, while the mountains provide a home for birds like the ptarmigan and the snow bunting. Secondly, the sea around Lofoten is rich in food resources, supporting a large and diverse population of small animals and fish. This larder provides plenty of food for millions of seabirds, not only in the colonies but also for the birds nesting on islets and islands.

What follows is a brief survey of the most prominent species, which should all be easy to spot and tell apart. Remember that a trip to Lofoten and Vesterålen will always be incomplete if you have not experienced bird colonies at close range. Get in touch with the local tourist information office for details on guided tours.

Next page: The kittiwake is a frequent sight and easily spotted by its lemon-colored bill. Young birds are often slow to find a mate and a nesting site, instead gathering in little clubs on the skerries and hoping for better luck next year.

The eider is the most common duck in the region, and some down is still collected, although the practice has lost its economic significance.

Eider

The eider is unquestionably the most common species of duck in the area, often referred to as the national bird of the coastland. Everywhere you'll see small flocks of this fairly large duck, in summer frequently one or two females with their young in tow. The male has distinct black and white markings, while the female is of a more uniformly brown color, so the two are easy to tell apart. The nest is often concealed and lined with the famous eider down, which the birds pluck from their own chests. It rates among the most effective insulating materials known to man and is unrivalled in sleeping bags and comforters. In earlier times the gathering of down afforded coastal residents an important extra income, and it was often necessary to visit from fifty to

sixty nests to collect a couple of pounds of down. The eider was so highly valued, both for its eggs and the down, that many people built small stone or wooden houses on their islets in order to attract as many eider females as possible. Today the collection of down is practically a thing of the past. Eiders like company, so you often see two or three females that have merged their broods, thus achieving better protection against predators.

Kittiwake

One of the handsomest and most frequently seen gulls is the kittiwake. It is very tame and often builds nests on wharfside warehouses, in windowsills, and in other locations near human habitation. The largest numbers are, however, found on the cliffs.

The kittiwake is easily recognized by its characteristic sharp cry, a greenish-yellow or nearly lemon-colored bill, black legs, and wholly black wingtips. It is a skilled flyer and maneuvers by means of small, neat movements. This gull is a typical migratory bird, arriving from the ocean in March or April; and the pairs, often in lifelong partnerships, return to the same cliff and often the same nest year after year.

The nest is more elaborate than that of other gulls and is made of damp grass, seaweeds, clay, soil, and the bird's own droppings. The soggy materials ensure that the nest is well anchored onto rock walls and other exposed sites. It also means that the kittiwake can establish a foothold where no one else has the courage or the ability to do so. The birds take turns incubating their two eggs, as well as caring for their young.

In October the kittiwakes all leave Norway and live on the open sea. Some go as far as the coast of Greenland or Canada. Immature birds may stay on the ocean as long as three years before returning to their childhood colony. There they live as singles for a year or two before establishing a partnership, building a nest, and laying eggs. This long period of preparation may be needed to master the often complicated and busy life in a bird colony.

Right: The great black-backed gull is among our largest gulls.

As a rule the kittiwake nests in colonies, sharing guard duty for mutual protection. The nest, consisting of sticky seaweed and grass, is practically glued onto the rock wall, a practice that gives great population density even on precipitous rockfaces.

The herring gull is large and adaptible. Its food consists of sea urchins, fish offal and other waste material.

Left: The common gull readily adjusts to civilization, and this one has picked an untraditional building site.

Great and Lesser Black-Backed Gull

If you see a gull that has a completely black topside, it is either a lesser black-backed gull or a great black-backed gull. The latter is our largest gull and has gray feet, while the lesser black-backed gull is smaller, shaplier, and has bright yellow legs. Both breed in colonies on skerries and promontories, but never on the cliffs. The latter are too steep; and since both of these gulls act as birds of prey when given the chance, they would promptly be ousted from the cliffs as soon as they tried. Both gulls lay rather large eggs, previously gathered for human consumption. Many adult great black-backed gulls

stay the winter on the coast, while younger birds go south to the North Sea and the coasts of the European continent. The lesser black-backed gull is a true bird of passage. It winters in south-western Europe and northern Africa, arrives in Lofoten only in April or May, and leaves the area again in September or October. All the black-backed gulls you see in the winter are therefore great black-backed gulls.

Herring Gull and Common Gull

Both of these gulls are white-bellied, have a silvery gray mantle and wings with a narrow black band almost at the tip. The herring gull is, however, considerably larger than the common gull, and it also has a strong yellow bill with a red spot near its base, while the common gull has a yellowish-green bill with no red spot. Like the great black-backed gull the herring gull frequently nests in colonies, and these are often mixed. The herring gull, however, adjusts far more readily to human presence and is not skittish. It appears in great numbers on garbage dumps, near fishing industry, and the like. It is fairly omnivorous, but crab, sea urchins, and mussels are at the top of the menu.

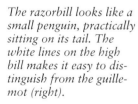

The razorbill looks like a small penguin, practically sitting on its tail. The white lines on the high bill makes it easy to distinguish from the guillemot (right).

Aside from the pointed, dark bill, the guillemot resembles the razorbill. Both lay only one egg and place it directly on the rock without protection.

The sea urchins are often lifted high into the air and dropped onto rocky surfaces, where they are broken, allowing the meal to be consumed. The herring gull can also act as a thief on occasion. It will for instance attack ducks surfacing after a dive and scare them into dropping their prey. The common gull eats small animals and fish found along the shore and shows little aggression towards other birds. However, if you unexpectedly get too close to the

nest, you will find that there is considerable temper in this little bird.

In both species older birds often winter at home, while younger ones lacking experience fly south to the North Sea when winter darkness and snow set in.

Razorbill and Guillemot

The razorbill and the guillemot both look like miniature penguins in their upright posture with legs placed far back on the body. In their breeding places the birds often rest on their tails and use the legs only for support. The guillemot has a long, sharp pitch-black bill, while the razorbill has a much deeper bill with two white stripes, one running lengthwise, the other crosswise. The guillemot breeds only on cliffs and lays its eggs right onto the rock or among a few paltry twigs. If the bird is frightened, the egg often rolls off the edge. The egg is in fact noticeably

pointed, which tends to make it turn on its own axis rather than roll along. This is a nice adaptation for a bird that hatches on narrow rock ledges. The razorbill, on the other hand, breeds mostly in caves or among rocks and is thus better protected. Both dive for fish in fairly deep water, plunging to depths of a hundred and fifty feet.

The razorbill generally ventures no farther than a few miles out for fish, while the guillemot may go as far as thirty miles offshore in search of suitable fishing grounds harboring herring and capelin.

Atlantic Puffin

The puffin is also an auk, but it is so extraordinary that it deserves a separate description. It is easily recognized because of its red-striped broad gray bill, a large white area around the eye, and its red legs. No wonder it is often called a sea parrot. The puffin is a migratory bird, moving onshore in April and laying its single egg well into rockfall crevices or in burrows dug into the ground. The birds form life partnerships and usually return to the same place for the rest of their lives, which is a long time: twenty or thirty years is not an uncommon life span for a puffin. The egg is incubated for forty days, and the nestling remains in the burrow for nearly two months before it is forced to get out onto the ocean simply because the parents starve it out. The puffin is an avid flyer and often travels as far as thirty or sixty miles offshore in search of good fishing grounds. It is totally dependent on sprat, so the disappearance of the latter results in mass extinction in the colonies, and this indeed happened in the eighties. The puffin is a popular prey, and many gulls and jaegers keep an eye on the puffin colonies and attack the weary birds on their return from the sea. The

The cormorants are a common sight in Lofoten and Vesterålen. The heavy birds fly low over the water or spend hours keeping watch.

great black-backed gull seizes adults, especially in strong winds, when the short-winged puffin has trouble maneuvering.

Cormorant

The cormorants have always had an aura of mystery about them, sitting som- ber and taciturn on the outermost reefs; and there are many tales and legends about these birds. The common, or great, cormorant can most easily be rec- ognized by a white spot on its thigh and a gray throat. The shag, or green cor- morant, is completely black; and in spring it is easily spotted by a tuft of feathers sticking up like a rooster's comb on top of the head. Both build large nests, using seaweeds, often located in rockfalls or between large boulders, fre- quently at the bottom of the bird cliffs. The cormorants fly low over the water and are unwieldy in their movements. One reason is their weight, in the case of the great cormorant often close to eight pounds; another is the placement of the wings far to the back on the long body. But then it is under water that they are

truly in their element. Speeds of up to six yards per second have been recorded, and even fast swimmers like the mackerel prove to be an easy prey.

The cormorants have poorly waxed wings, so after diving they may spread their wings and remain immobile for hours in order to dry them.

Gray Sea Eagle

The most impressive bird you find out here is the gray sea eagle, and it appears in greater numbers in Lofoten and Vesterålen than anywhere else. Out at Værøy I had the experience of looking down at eight of these birds soundlessly shearing through the air below me. The reasons for their great numbers are an abundance of steep rock walls suitable for nests, and a rich food supply.

The gray sea eagle is a large, majestic bird with a wingspan of almost six feet. It is a memorable experience to watch these birds against the sky, gliding on the wind and making wide circles in their hunt for prey. Adult birds are non-migratory, so you can see eagles all year out here. Eagles are protected by law and are now on the increase.

Oyster Catcher

The most common wader in Lofoten and Vesterålen is the oyster catcher. You find it wherever there is a beach or an intertidal shore. Its bright red legs and bill, its black head and back, its white breast and sharp trilling call make it our most easily recognizable wader. It is a bird of passage and arrives as early as February or March,

The numerous gray sea eagles in the region live on birds, fish, and carrion. The great wingspan makes the bird one of our stateliest.

The tern is one of our most skilled fliers, migrating all the way to South Africa in the winter. It has a temper and will attack without fear if you get too close to the nest.

The oyster catcher is easily spotted with its scarlet legs and its characteristic shrill call.

Above right: The fulmar uses Værøy and Røst primarily for nesting, spending the rest of the year on the open sea. The long nostrils on top of the bill make it easy to recognize.

Right: The heron, our largest wader, nests in small colonies throughout the archipelago. It feeds on small fish and animals found on the seashore and along brooks and lakes.

so the sound of the oyster catcher is always a welcome sign of spring along the coast. The nest, containing three eggs, is placed quite randomly on the ground, and the male and the female, joined in a lifelong partnership, take turns brooding. In the fall they leave for southern Europe, and young birds stay there for as long as four or five years before finding a mate. If you notice small "clubs" of oyster catchers on the beach, bickering and scolding one another, they are often such young birds getting ready for the serious business of adulthood.

FISHES

Nowhere else in Norway is the fishing as abundant as in Lofoten and Vesterålen. The well-known Lofoten Fishery in winter was instrumental in humans settling in this area, but it was also important to the coastal population throughout northern Norway. Besides cod and coalfish there are numerous other species of fish in the sea here. If your visit includes Kabelvåg at Austvågøy, the aquarium there would be just the place for learning about them. You are free to fish from skerries, rocky shores, and wharfs; but if you want bigger fish, you have to take up deep-sea fishing. The best way to do that is to rent a boat or to join organized fishing trips led by experienced fishermen. Stop by the local tour-

Among the region's numerous fish species cod and coalfish, or pollack, predominate. Fishing is the primary source of income, above all cod fishing.

Fishing is done from all kinds of vessels - from small boats to commercial vessels where the fish is partially processed before landing.

ist information office to find out about the options available to you.

Cod

This is unquestionably the most important fish in this part of the country, and it is the mainstay of the Lofoten Fishery. Already from around the year 700 we have sources referring to ships that sailed all the way to England in the summer, carrying fish products that were traded for grain, textiles, and implements. Boats from all along the Norwegian coast took part in the annual fishing bonanza, which involved as many as 20,000 fishermen each year, and in boom seasons the catch exceeded 140,000 tons.

The basis for the Lofoten Fishery is the Barents Sea codfish population. In December the seven to ten-year-old spawning-ready cod begins migrating from there down along the Norwegian coast. Breeding takes place all along the coastline to Møre, but the greatest activity occurs on the inside of the Lofoten islands. The water temperature governs the cod's arrival at Lofoten and Vesterålen around January or February. The impetus for all this cod to seek out this particular area lies in a combination of the "warm" water from the Gulf Stream and the plentiful supply of food.

A single female cod has approximately five million eggs in her body, and she spawns around twenty times in the course of a month and a half. Spawning takes place at depths of fifty to a hundred yards, and following fertilization the eggs slowly rise to the surface. After three weeks the eggs are hatched, and then the cod larvae must fend for themselves. Naturally most of the eggs and the young succumb as nutriment for other fish. The survivors float slowly along in the northward current to the Barents Sea, a voyage of two to three years. The cod not harvested during the winter also returns to the Barents Sea and the area around Svalbard, and may make several of these breeding migrations in the course of a lifetime.

In earlier days nearly all of the fish was dried, and this method of preservation is still important, as shown by the large number of drying racks all along this part of the coast. The combination of cold and dry air assures prime drying conditions and gives protection against insects and other pests; in spring the fish is taken down and shipped south to the European continent. Today much of the fish is processed in the many fish processing plants, being frozen, salted, smoked, or prepared to be sold fresh.

In addition to cod from the Barents Sea there are local cod populations in Lofoten and Vesterålen, the so-called fjord cod. This is normally the kind summer visitors get to know. Such fjord cod seldom exceeds twenty or thirty pounds, while a full-grown cod may reach some eighty pounds. The cod is easy to spot with the characteristic barbel under its chin and the curved lateral line.

Coalfish

The coalfish, or pollack, is also a codfish, but it is slimmer and has a distinctly silvery body and a straight lateral line running from the head to the tail. The coalfish typically travels in schools and

Today's sophisticated fishing methods require a fisheries inspection service to ensure that resources are nor depleted or unfairly distributed.

Above left: Cod and coalfish supply professional and sport fishermen alike with their most important catch.

Left: Redfish is a deep-water fish caught only in nets.

Salmon farming plays an important role all along the Norwegian coast. The country produces more than 300,000 tons of salmon annually. Plenty of never-freezing saltwater makes the Norwegian coast ideal for aquaculture.

Many people come to Lofoten and Vesterålen for sport fishing or to stock the larder. You would have to be a pretty pitiful fisherman not to catch anything here. This American clearly shows his enthusiasm!

is constantly on the move. Breeding takes place in deep water, and eggs and fry drift north with the coastal currents. In contrast to the cod, the young coalfish finds a home in the shallow coastal waters.

Coalfish hunt for all kinds of fish, and they often surround schools of herrings or sprats, which are forced to the surface as the coalfish plunge into the food. The prey leaps into the air in a desperate attempt to escape. In minutes the gulls descend on the area to claim their share of the feast, giving the local fisherman a sure sign of coalfish in the fjord. Next to cod and herring the coalfish is our most important fish, and some years Norwegian fishermen land more than 100,000 tons of coalfish, much of it in Lofoten and Vesterålen.

A hard-fighting fully grown coalfish is a challenge to the most finicky of anglers, and since it tends to move near the surface and is greedy and eager to bite, it often provides even modestly equipped visitors with a generous catch.